SHARKS SET I

TIGER SHARKS

Heidi Mathea
ABDO Publishing Company

visit us at
www.abdopublishing.com

Published by ABDO Publishing Company, 8000 West 78th Street, Edina, Minnesota 55439. Copyright © 2011 by Abdo Consulting Group, Inc. International copyrights reserved in all countries. No part of this book may be reproduced in any form without written permission from the publisher. The Checkerboard Library™ is a trademark and logo of ABDO Publishing Company.

Printed in the United States of America, North Mankato, Minnesota.
042010
092010

 PRINTED ON RECYCLED PAPER

Cover Photo: © Jon Cornforth/SeaPics.com
Interior Photos: Alamy p. 17; © James D. Watt/SeaPics.com p. 19;
     © John Morrissey/SeaPics.com p. 15; © Masa Ushioda/SeaPics.com pp. 4–5;
     Peter Arnold pp. 6, 8, 11, 13, 21; Uko Gorter pp. 7, 9

Editor: Megan M. Gunderson
Art Direction & Cover Design: Neil Klinepier

Library of Congress Cataloging-in-Publication Data

Mathea, Heidi, 1979-
  Tiger sharks / Heidi Mathea.
       p. cm. -- (Sharks)
  Includes index.
  ISBN 978-1-61613-429-7
  1. Tiger shark--Juvenile literature. 2. Tiger shark. I. Title.

QL638.95.C3M38 2011
597.3'4--dc22

                                        2010007287

CONTENTS

TIGER SHARKS AND FAMILY 4

WHAT THEY LOOK LIKE 6

WHERE THEY LIVE 8

FOOD 10

SENSES 12

BABIES 14

ATTACK AND DEFENSE 16

ATTACKS ON HUMANS 18

TIGER SHARK FACTS 20

GLOSSARY 22

WEB SITES 23

INDEX 24

TIGER SHARKS AND FAMILY

Sharks are some of the most feared creatures swimming in the world's waters. They are among the top predators of the sea. Today, there are more than 400 species of sharks. Sharks come in various sizes, shapes, and colors.

All sharks are fish covered in small, toothlike scales called denticles. This rough layer protects their skin. Sharks also have skeletons made of cartilage. This is the same substance that makes up the human ear.

Tiger sharks are one of the most dangerous sharks to man. They are usually slow swimmers. But, they will move fast to catch prey. This species is known for its interesting diet. Tiger sharks will try anything, including people!

The tiger shark belongs to the family Carcharhinidae.

What They Look Like

The tiger shark's name comes from the tigerlike stripes and spots on its skin. These markings fade as the shark ages. The tiger shark is bluish green to dark gray or black on top. Its belly is yellowish white to white.

The tiger shark has a robust head. It features two large eyes and five gill slits on each side of the head. The **blunt** snout contains a wide mouth armed with sharp, **serrated** teeth.

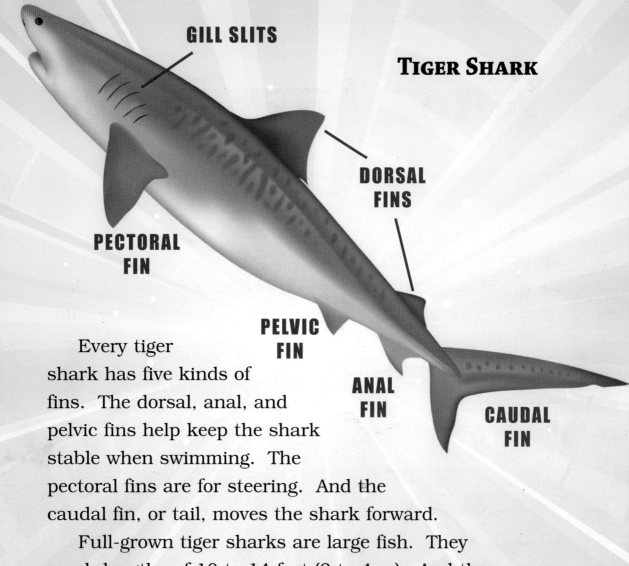

GILL SLITS

TIGER SHARK

DORSAL FINS

PECTORAL FIN

PELVIC FIN

ANAL FIN

CAUDAL FIN

Every tiger shark has five kinds of fins. The dorsal, anal, and pelvic fins help keep the shark stable when swimming. The pectoral fins are for steering. And the caudal fin, or tail, moves the shark forward.

Full-grown tiger sharks are large fish. They reach lengths of 10 to 14 feet (3 to 4 m). And they weigh 850 to 1,400 pounds (390 to 640 kg). Their size alone demands respect.

WHERE THEY LIVE

Tiger sharks are found worldwide. They live in all **temperate** and **tropical** waters, except the Mediterranean Sea. Tiger sharks are often seen close to the water's surface. However, they may also dive as deep as 1,150 feet (350 m).

These fierce sharks prefer to live in murky coastal waters. They are common in

In the wild, tiger sharks can live up to 50 years.

Where Do Tiger Sharks Live?

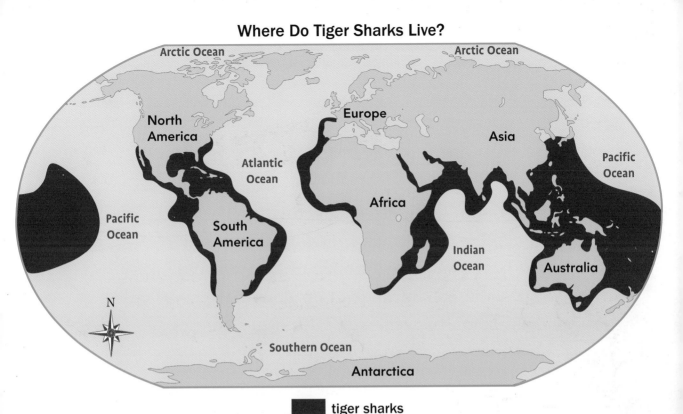

tiger sharks

lagoons, river **estuaries**, and harbors. Tiger sharks have also been spotted far offshore.

As the seasons change, tiger sharks **migrate**. During warmer months, they move from **tropical** to **temperate** waters. They return to warm waters in winter.

FOOD

Tiger sharks like to feed at night. They often hunt alone. Sometimes they form loose schools when there is a large amount of food around.

These fierce sharks feed on bony fish, rays, sea snakes, dolphins, seabirds, and other sharks. Tiger sharks also eat armored prey such as sea turtles.

But, tiger sharks are really known for the junk they consume. A variety of human items have been found in their stomachs. This includes tin cans, clothing, plastic bottles, and burlap sacks. None of this junk is good for these sharks. They just eat anything they can swallow!

The tiger shark is nicknamed "wastebasket of the sea."

SENSES

The tiger shark's many well-developed senses make it a dangerous predator. Its large eyes see well in dim water. This amazing fish also has a good sense of smell. If prey is injured or bleeding, a tiger shark can locate it from a long distance.

Like all sharks, the tiger shark senses the weak electric fields all living animals give off. This is achieved with a system of sense **organs** around the shark's head. This sense may lead a tiger shark to its next meal. It also helps the shark navigate.

In addition, sharks have excellent hearing. They use their ears and lateral line systems to detect sounds and vibrations. The lateral line consists of sense organs along each shark's body. Using these sensitive systems tells sharks about their surroundings.

The tiger shark has a third eyelid. When the shark goes in for the attack, this eyelid closes to protect the eye.

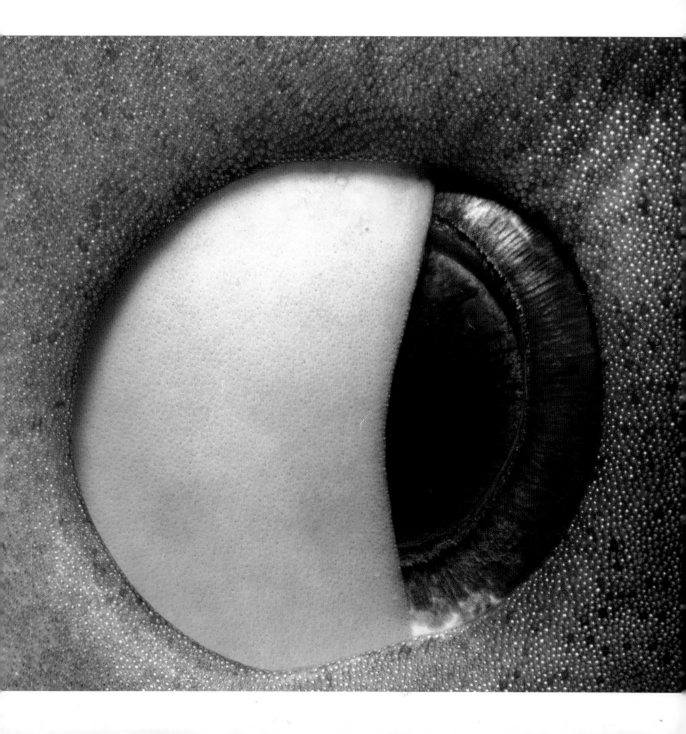

BABIES

A baby tiger shark begins life inside its mother as an egg. Instead of laying her eggs, the mother shark carries them inside her. There, the eggs hatch after 14 to 16 months. Soon after, the baby sharks are born live. A mother tiger shark gives birth to 10 to 80 baby sharks. The babies are called pups.

Tiger shark pups are 12 to 18 inches (31 to 46 cm) long at birth. Once they are born, the pups are on their own. Luckily, they are fully developed and able to swim.

Newborn tiger sharks have many predators to fear. Even larger tiger sharks will eat them! The young sharks use their strong senses to hunt and survive.

Most shark mothers give birth in special nursery areas located in shallow water.

ATTACK AND DEFENSE

A tiger shark's teeth are its greatest weapons. They are made to snag and cut prey. There is not much these sharp teeth can't saw into!

Shark teeth grow in rows. When a tooth breaks or falls out, a new one replaces it. The dangerous tiger shark's large mouth is filled with teeth! There are about 24 teeth in every row.

Size and fierceness are a tiger shark's greatest defenses. An adult tiger shark has little to fear except man. Fishermen are eager to catch these sharks for their fins, flesh, and skin. Tiger sharks are also caught for sport.

Tiger sharks can get moving fast when they smell something tasty!

ATTACKS ON HUMANS

The tiger shark is one of the most dangerous sharks to man. Only the great white shark has been involved in more attacks on humans. From 1580 to 2006, there were 145 tiger shark attacks.

Tiger sharks don't hunt humans. Yet, they are curious when they encounter divers and swimmers. And they can be **aggressive**. Humans should always respect these fierce sharks.

To help prevent a shark attack, follow a few rules. If you are bleeding, get out of the water. Sharks are attracted to the smell of blood. Also, avoid swimming in murky waters. Tiger sharks prefer these areas.

Follow these rules and remain aware of your surroundings. This will keep the oceans safe for you and the sharks.

Remember, tiger sharks are large and deadly. Open water diving is not for inexperienced divers.

Tiger Shark Facts

Scientific Name:

Tiger shark   *Galeocerdo cuvier*

Average Size:

Tiger sharks are 10 to 14 feet (3 to 4 m) long.

Where They're Found:

Tiger sharks live worldwide in temperate and tropical waters, except the Mediterranean Sea.

The largest tiger sharks on record were more than 17 feet (5.5 m) long. They weighed more than 2,000 pounds (900 kg)!

GLOSSARY

aggressive (uh-GREH-sihv) - displaying hostility.

blunt - rounded.

estuary (EHS-chuh-wehr-ee) - the area of water where a river's current meets an ocean's tide.

migrate - to move from one place to another, often to find food.

organ - a part of an animal or a plant composed of several kinds of tissues. An organ performs a specific function. The heart, liver, gallbladder, and intestines are organs of an animal.

serrated - notched like a saw.

temperate - relating to an area where average temperatures range between 50 and 55 degrees Fahrenheit (10 and 13°C).

tropical - relating to an area with an average temperature above 77 degrees Fahrenheit (25°C) where no freezing occurs.

WEB SITES

To learn more about tiger sharks, visit ABDO Publishing Company on the World Wide Web at **www.abdopublishing.com**. Web sites about tiger sharks are featured on our Book Links page. These links are routinely monitored and updated to provide the most current information available.

INDEX

A

attacks 5, 18

B

belly 6
body 6, 7, 12

C

cartilage 5
color 6

D

defense 5, 14, 16
denticles 5

E

ears 12
eggs 14
environment 8, 9,
    18
eyes 6, 12

F

fins 7, 16
food 5, 10, 12, 16

G

gill slits 6

H

head 6, 12
hunting 10, 12, 14

L

lateral line 12

M

migration 9
mouth 6, 16

P

predators 14, 16
pups 14

R

reproduction 14

S

schools 10
senses 12, 14
shark species 4
size 7, 14, 16
skin 5, 6, 16
snout 6

T

tail 7
teeth 6, 16